Finding Your Way

The Art of Natural Navigation

Jennifer Owings Dewey
Photographs by Stephen Trimble

THE MILLBROOK PRESS
BROOKFIELD, CONNECTICUT

Library of Congress Cataloging-in-Publication Data
Dewey, Jennifer.
Finding your way : the art of natural navigation / Jennifer Owings Dewey.
    p. cm.
Includes bibliographical references (p.).
ISBN 0-7613-0956-X (lib. bdg.)
1. Wilderness survival—Juvenile literature. 2. Orienteering—Juvenile literature.
[1. Wilderness survival. 2. Orienteering. 3. Survival.] 1. Title.
GV200.5.D48   2001
795.58—dc21   00-032893

Published by The Millbrook Press, Inc.
2 Old New Milford Road
Brookfield, Connecticut 06804

Photographs, except for pages 18, 19, 21, and 55 copyright © 2001 by Stephen
Trimble; pp. 18, 21, and 55 copyright © 2001 by Jennifer Owings Dewey; p. 19
courtesy of Giraudon/Art Resource, NY

Contents

Introduction

Once, Jennifer Owings Dewey told me about a time when she was young and ran away from home. No matter how far she walked, she couldn't feel lost. She knew where the ranch on which she lived was located, she knew the mountains that rose hazy in the distance, and she knew the plants at her feet and the occasional animal that scurried past. Even sharing a cave with bats she felt safe. She knew where she was.

I think about the places I know well. Forty years later, I can imagine going to the house where I grew up. I know the foyer, the tiles on the floor, and the height of the ceiling. I can do this mental wandering through the rooms of my grandmother's apartment in New York City, in the store where my father worked, and around a farmhouse in Wisconsin. But I know that some people have a different sense of place.

On that farm in Wisconsin, for instance, I know where the apple trees are located and where water collects in the spring floods. But there was an old man up the road who could tell you where the sun rose and set at different times of the year. Having a personalized sense of geography is surely about place, but it also has to do with time.

Jennifer Dewey's sense of personal geography integrates time and space. Is this something that all earthbound inhabitants can develop?

There are, of course, tricks for finding your way. From the highest point you can glimpse the surrounding terrain and re-establish your bearings. Always notice where the sun rises and sets. Remain aware of what features are on your right and which are on your left as you walk an unknown trail. Notice how water flows. But these are the bits of advice found in lots of books on orienteering.

What Ms. Dewey tells us in the following pages is how it feels to be lost and have time and space intersect to give us clues and help us regain our confidence and a centered feeling that, yes, it's going to be all right.

As human beings, and yet part of the animal world, we constantly identify structures and natural rhythms that enable us to survive. But when we are away from our familiar landscape, this becomes a challenge. As I write this, I think of escaped slaves, making their way north. No compass but the stars, no map but a song with coded directions to provide a clue that they are on the right track. The first adventurers to travel a new route must have felt that same sense of knowing and yet not knowing, faith winning out over fear.

These stories are an understated tribute to the ability of humans, born without so many of the instincts common to other animals, to venture into the world. From now on, whenever I find myself disoriented—in the desert, lost in a field of tall corn, confused at an airport—I will think of these stories and smile. The clues are there, I will tell myself. Stop. Take note. Where is there movement? How can I work with this time and place, rather than against it? Clearly there is pleasure in being lost and then finding yourself, if only because you can then release the draining fear that accompanies not knowing. For those like Jennifer Dewey who have challenged themselves on so many fronts, thank you for sharing your adventures. Thank you for taking us along.

—Wendy Saul

The name Jornada del Muerto, spanish for "dead man's journey," refers to the experience of a German trader accused of witchcraft who, in 1670, escaped from prison and into the Jornada. His sun-dried corpse was discovered years later.

Walking on the Jornada del Muerto Desert

It's not on any map——no true places ever are.
MARK TWAIN

There are no roads in the Jornada, only cow trails studded with tire-popping volcanic rocks. I wrestled a four-wheel-drive vehicle across this rough, dry desert in New Mexico for seventy miles, the only sign of human presence an occasional windmill, a slender sentinel breaking the monotony of the nearly flat landscape. Rusty stock tanks riddled with bullet holes squat near the bottoms of the windmills, the slimy water surface buzzing with insects.

I came alone to the lava flats in the desert. I wanted to explore a cave where a colony of Mexican freetail bats, all females, spends the summer raising bat babies. A biologist friend who had been to the cave scrawled directions for me, and I set off.

After reaching the cave, I spent the afternoon and evening crawling around in the cavity that is home to the bats. The cave air is rank with the stench of ammonia from bat urine and hazy from shed fur. Baby bats slip silently to the cave floor, to be devoured in minutes by dermestid beetles.

I left the cave early the next morning. Shortly after starting for the highway, an uneven rut threw my truck into a boulder. The axle was broken.

I stood paralyzed by the ruined truck, flooded with disbelief at what had happened. I was stranded and would have to walk out on foot. A wind like hot stale breath pushed against me. I wanted to cry out, "Don't leave me all alone out here!"

I tried to focus on where I was. Because I was on foot I could strike north, a shortcut impossible with the truck. I hoped to intersect the main road, a distance of about fifty miles.

Two distant mountain ranges, one in the east, another in the west, helped me figure direction. I knew if I walked between the two ranges I would be going north. If I made the mistake of turning south I would face many miles of waterless desert clear into Mexico.

For hours, until it collapsed in the dirt, I followed a fence line, droopy strands of barbed wire stapled to weathered posts. To save energy I went slowly and stopped often. My head swirled with

Traveling in the desert in summer heat can make a person disoriented due to extreme temperatures and lack of water. Once a foot traveler has become dehydrated, confusion sets in. The same happens when a traveler is tired, not paying attention, or distracted by hunger and thirst. It is important to rest frequently, to be aware of, and to conserve energy.

doubts about surviving the July heat with half a canteen of water. Alone and scared, I was struck by the immense loneliness of desert space and silence.

I said prayers for survival and prayers that I'd have sense enough to keep north and not go in circles.

Desert heat adds to a traveler's confusion by creating mirages. I thought I saw mountain ranges covered with snow, pools of bright blue water, sea waves, images floating in the distance that looked real but were vapor, not real at all.

A pattern of sound penetrated my brain, a symphony of noises from desert-dwelling animals. Gradually I began to notice what was happening around me.

A mirage is created when light rays pass from one layer of air to another, one layer cold, the other warm. The speed of the passing light rays is altered, and the rays are bent (refracted), so they strike the eye from a direction different from their point of origin. Light rays passing through layers of air often create shimmering pools of blue, even on sunbaked pavement, giving the impression of water where none exists.

Black grasshoppers bumped against my legs and ankles, fat green flies buzzed like heavy bombers on dark wings, white moths fluttered over dry stems. A wasp dove for a red ant closing in on a tiny beetle running for its life.

I became obsessed with minutiae. Focusing on tiny helped clear my mind. A tarantula walked on the sand, leaving a delicate trail of claw marks in its wake. The spider lifted hairy legs and set them down with ballet-like precision. I brushed the tarantula's back with a cactus spine. It hesitated, then went on. The indifference of the tarantula to my pestering was oddly reassuring.

A snake of a species unknown to me slipped by. Rosy-scaled and skinny as a rope, it seemed to levitate over the ground and not touch down.

"Where are you going?" I asked. "If you're headed for water, take me with you."

I gently poked a carrion beetle with a twig of sagebrush. Two inches long, with smooth, shiny wing covers, it reacted by standing on its head. I gently knocked it over, and it righted itself. Whether the beetle knew which trail to take, it knew where to put its clawed feet.

Many animals, from birds to bacteria, have organs that help them navigate. The hunting spider (Cupiennius salei) has directional organs in its legs. Animals such as gerbils, lobsters, crabs, and millipedes have internal compasses that help them compensate for changes in wind and water direction.

Many finding-the-way organs involve the inner ear. Humans with poor inner-ear structure (often caused by disease) suffer vertigo—a condition in which a person feels that his or her surroundings are whirling about.

I thought of how the first human travelers in the desert had found their way across windswept dunes from one oasis to the next. Ancient traders surely used the sun by day, and the stars by night, establishing long-lasting trade routes. I looked for game trails running north. Small herds of antelope cross the Jornada, following often, if not always, the shortest routes.

Any true sense of where I was in space and time was distorted by my fear. I panicked and lost north and had to stop and locate it again. I wasted good energy being angry. The stony, cactus-strewn land made me furious. I was no match for the harsh country, not tough enough. My lips, tongue, and throat were swollen from thirst, my skin bright red, blistered by the sun.

I scared up a covey of quail. They buzzed away with top-knot feathers quivering, horrified at being caught in the open, startled by a looming intruder. The little birds seemed too delicate for the desert, fragile and soft in contrast to the harsh landscape. I thought of my own obvious fragility.

It is impossible to imagine what being stranded and "lost" feels like. Exhaustion makes you wonder how your legs are going to keep you standing, to say nothing of walking. Every joint aches. Hunger makes you stagger. Thirst makes you want to create moisture in your mouth, but you can't produce any saliva.

A beetle trail and the prints of a kangaroo rat marked a patch of sand. These animals never drink. All the moisture they need is in their food. They rarely urinate, excreting tiny, brownish, concentrated droplets three or four times in their lives.

After many hours of walking, I began to "see" leaping, charging snakes and a dancer with feathers on his head, and I knew I was hallucinating, suffering the early stages of heat stroke. I found a patch of shade and took a nap.

When I was up and moving again, I thought: Antelope and coyote live out here, why not me, for a few hours at least?

"Just passing through," I said, addressing a brittle shaft of ocatilla.

My feet kicked up dry seedpods with weird shapes, containers for new life. One looked like a miniature goat's head with prickly spines. Dry brown grass leaned away from the wind, falling on the ground like strands of hair. The grass looked defeated, and I could not imagine it ever being green.

I yearned for rain, and knew by the bright, cloudless sky that none was in the making. Westerlies, the prevailing winds, brought only warm air blowing over the ground.

Toward evening Swainson's hawks appeared in the sky. I became tearfully awash (dry tears) with admiration and envy. If you are a hawk and take a notion to fly fifteen miles to water you do—simple as that.

Many desert plants store water in taproots. Sucking or chewing on these roots provides some relief from thirst.

Dark shadows grew across the land, and the western horizon turned pink and blue. A thick brown haze, the last of a far-off dust storm, drifted like smoke. Fire-red clouds lit by the sun's last light promised relief from the heat.

When the moon was high, the night turned cold. I scratched out a spot and burrowed into the sand like a horned lizard seeking warmth.

Morning came with the calls of doves, low and soft, like women weeping in a graveyard. I woke up amazed to have slept. Butterflies were everywhere in the heavy, warm air.

I set off north and saw a windmill ahead. Windmills mean a chance of water.

A scummy water hole surrounded the base of the windmill, leakage from the tank. I dared not drink.

A metal ladder was bolted to the rusted legs of the windmill. I climbed to the top, sat on a rickety platform of weathered wood, and looked north. The two-lane paved highway was visible in the distance. I knew that I would reach it before falling face down dead of thirst and heat in the sand.

Standing at the roadside, I felt a pang of sadness at leaving the desert. So much of my time had been consumed in feeling angry and afraid. I'd missed chances to revel in the experience. I wished I could go back and do it over, do it right.

Water holes or stock tanks on the desert may be poisoned, not by pollution but by dead animals or toxic natural minerals. It is unwise to chance drinking such water. Boiling, using filtering tablets, or adding iodine cleans water and makes it drinkable.

A car whooshed past and screeched to a halt. It backed up and stopped where I stood. A woman in a tattered straw hat and a pretty summer dress was behind the wheel. She had the windows open. Dust swirled inside the car like sea fog.

"You are *filthy*," she said, staring at me. "You been living underground?"

She took me to town, where I drank gallons of lemonade and had an endless bath before finding someone to help me rescue my truck.

For some, finding the way in the wilderness is an addiction. A need to leave civilization, to explore and discover new territory, runs deep in many human souls. The time I spent on the desert led me to another wilderness—Antarctica.

Penguin Country

I'm just going outside and may be some time.
TITUS OATS

I dreamed for years of going to Antarctica. In my imagination Antarctica was mysterious, a wilderness where myths are born. Myths are often dispelled when you experience what you've dreamed about. They can be made the same way.

The Antarctic wilderness, penguin country, satisfies the expectations of the most demanding adventurer. Remote, breathtakingly beautiful, its

Antarctica is an ice desert, the coldest, driest, windiest place on earth. It is the fifth-largest continent and covers ten percent of the earth's surface, stretching nearly five-and-one-half million square miles and containing two-thirds of the world's supply of fresh water.

vast stretches of glacier ice present physical challenges unparalleled anywhere except in outer space.

Antarctica appears to be all ice and snow, a white, cold world. It is known as "the white land," and yet a brilliant range of colors can be seen there, delicate pinks, deep reds, vivid greens, lavenders, and intense blues. There is unexpected beauty in this stark, bold wilderness.

Titus Oats was with the English explorer Robert Falcon Scott on Scott's fatal journey to the South Pole. "Some time" turned out to be forever. Along with Scott and several others, Oats perished returning from the Pole, eleven miles from the coast and safety.

Why travel to the ends of the earth to suffer bitter and terrible hardships, to face the possibility of never coming home again?

Human curiosity demands exploration. Adventuring is essential for the health of the human spirit. People go into the unknown to rediscover their primeval selves, to make deep connections with nature, or to risk all for personal glory.

Among the people staying in the Antarctic with me was a New Zealander, a man who embodied the spirit of the old-time explorer. He might have been one, had he been born earlier. Many of the world's leg-

Early mappers did not know what lands or seas existed at the bottom of the earth. They had little or no knowledge of the positions of the continents. Terra incognita, Latin for unexplored or unknown land, is the name they gave to the Antarctic, or South Polar region. Mapmakers often decorated the area with sea monsters giving way to their imaginations.

endary adventurers, men like Edmond Hillary, first man to reach the summit of Everest, are native to New Zealand.

Having gone with no particular plan except to experience being there, I asked the New Zealander if I could join his expedition as an extra hand. He was a geologist working for the British Antarctic Survey, hired to map the area.

We went out nearly every day, loading a boat with gear for travel across water, or a sled to ride inland on glaciers. I was away from Base more than I was there.

A compass is a device for finding where true north is. The most basic compass is a magnetic needle that can pivot to align itself with magnetic north. The needle is inside a circular housing marked with the cardinal directions—east, west, north, and south.

True north is a cardinal point on a compass, the direction to the left of a person watching the rising sun.

Magnetic north is that point on the earth where magnetic fields converge. This point is often slightly different from true north.

In the early days of Antarctic exploration, men had one tool to find their way across a frozen landscape—a handheld spirit compass. They also remembered land forms, peninsulas jutting into the sea, distant mountains, the curve of a glacier, cove, bay, or ice cliff.

My New Zealander companion used landmarks of exposed granite rock, laid bare by fierce winds, to find and maintain a true course crossing water. One day we were exploring an island. He went in one direction and I in another. Fog drifted in, and before long I was disoriented, uncertain which way to go. The view in all directions was blotted out by thick mist. Hundreds of Adelie penguins nested on the island in a crowded rookery. I sat on a rock shelf wondering how to find the way to the boat. I heard penguin voices, which resemble donkeys braying, muffled but obvious in the background. I began to realize I knew where the rookery was in relation to the beach where the boat was. The calls of the penguins guided me.

Becoming a skilled way-finder means using your senses to gather information. Sensory messages in the environment are stored in your brain. Penguin voices were a clue for me to use. The direction of the wind, the smells in the air were more clues.

Later the New Zealander told me that by watching birds in flight, coming and going from sea to land, I would be able to orient myself. Seabirds, petrels, shearwaters, and albatross follow the same

There are seventeen different kinds of penguins. Common to the Antarctic region are Macaroni, Royal, King, Gentoo, Adelie, Emperor, and Chinstrap. Of these, only the Emperor and Adelie live in extremely cold areas all winter. The others migrate north to warmer seas, swimming for thousands of miles.

routes again and again. He himself shrugged off the use of a compass or other directional guide, sensing where he was in relation to where he wanted to go. He stood and watched the sea and ice-covered land, observing to remember, to mentally map physical details.

The New Zealander's sense of time was based on personal, private rhythms belonging to him alone. In a social setting clocks tick, bells

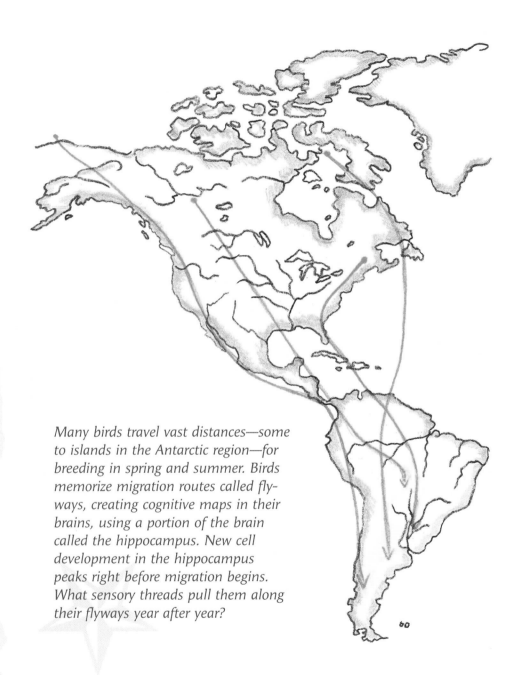

Many birds travel vast distances—some to islands in the Antarctic region—for breeding in spring and summer. Birds memorize migration routes called flyways, creating cognitive maps in their brains, using a portion of the brain called the hippocampus. New cell development in the hippocampus peaks right before migration begins. What sensory threads pull them along their flyways year after year?

ring, and daily activity is measured in minutes and hours. Not so for him; time had another meaning, a different feel.

I came to understand this one bright afternoon in January when I was alone on an island. I discovered a new way to experience the passage of time, unlike any other I'd known, more akin to the New Zealander's.

The island was patchy with orange lichens growing like fuzz on gray rocks. I lay on my stomach and gazed into the beady black eyes of an hours-old gull chick in the center of a nest heaped with feathers and dried seaweed. The chick, white down still damp from hatching, was inches from my nose. An invisible thread connected me to the chick, to the pulse of its life. My sense of time was the chick's. I was no longer separated by humanness.

Time exists in the wilderness, but not as it does in a civilized environment where the pace of life is constantly (and noisily) measured, where you cannot escape the beat of the hours.

In the wilderness time becomes a thread that is sensed. Heading out on a journey across a glacier, you imagine this thread leading you home. It is your sense of time passing that informs you of distance.

Invisible sensory threads connect whales cruising ocean depths. How they find their way eludes us. We listen to their songs and marvel at the mystery of what they mean. Are they sound maps that tell one whale where to find another?

I learned to find my way in fog, in thick soupy mist, and I learned to sense time passing, never mind a watch or even the sun to guide me.

A portion of the San
Juan River in southeast
Utah is designated as "wild and
scenic" by the federal government.
This means that stretches of the
river are protected from overuse.
Permits are required to run it,
and only a certain number of
permits are granted a year.
Everything river runners take
in must be brought out.

The Female
River Ghost

The river looked enormous, powerful, brown, the rubber
boats so fragile. I was scared, to tell the truth——
EDWARD ABBEY

"She was a female river ghost," the old man said.
He was a guide hired to take our party in rubber
rafts down the San Juan River in southern Utah.

"It's a rare thing, a she-ghost."

His whiskered face was creased, his hands
leathery. I pictured him always on one river or
another, never indoors.

"Tell us about her," someone said. My family, a few close friends, and I were all grouped around the campfire after supper, ready for a good story. The old man lit a cigar and began.

"I knew her family," he said. "River running was in her blood. Her mother and father were river guides all over the West. Her brothers got an early start at it. They all swore that any individual who didn't know a river by heart could not claim to know much of anything.

"She was an infant when she fell into the river the first time, wearing a diaper and an old canvas life jacket, the cotton padding thirsty as a goat. The family was on a trip on a river up north of here when she fell out of the lead raft, going in belly down, never making a sound. She bobbed along with her baby arms stuck out.

"You'd have thought she'd scream, but she did no such thing. Her grandfather grabbed her before she drowned. Marie Rose was what they named her, but she was called Ratonia from the start. The name shows no disrespect, it confirms the truth about the girl. She loved rivers as well as any river rat you can name.

"When she was still small, her daddy made certain she had her own boat. We ran the big ones together, the Colorado, the Salmon. She was as able as any boatman twice her size.

"She never finished school, but her mamma made sure she knew her letters and numbers. She read a lot. Loved books, and she put words down on paper about rivers, poetry you'd call it.

"Her daddy taught her that the best way to learn the tricks of a river is to float in it chin deep. Let yourself be carried in the water. Give yourself over to it.

"You see the river close up, the animals living by it, the twists and turns, the manner in which the water riffles, eddies, and flows. A river is always going somewhere. You can count on the flow of the stream if you're lost.

"We all tried it. Ratonia went in like that every chance she got. She'd float for hours, even days, staying out all night when she was of age and on her own. If you wanted to know the heart and soul of a Western river you only need ask her. She knew the rapids, the crossings, even the geology. She could tell you about Triassic layers, Entrada and Navajo sandstone, and the Chinle formation. She'd tell stories over the campfire about what strange fishes swam in Permian seas millions of years past. It wasn't just old times she had knowledge of. She'd name the wildlife you see passing down these rivers today, whiptails, Gila monsters, water beetles, robber flies, the ring-tailed cats.

"She read up and learned the human history of the rivers, too, going way back in time with her yarns, telling stories about the Ancient Ones, the Anasazi, people

What Edward Abbey called "our local ravine," the Grand Canyon of the Colorado in northern Arizona, is a classic example of of how a river cuts into the earth exposing layers of rock through ages of time. One way to know a river is to observe the geologic record the river's flow reveals.

Having a true knowledge of the wilderness means knowing every detail of the whole of it, from plants and animals to human events that shaped the area's history.

who lived in these river canyons thousands of years ago. She was rare for how she knew this country."

The old man puffed on his cigar. The moon was up. Nighthawks cried with plaintive voices. Under the spell cast by the old river guide's voice, we waited anxiously to learn how a spirited young female river guide ended up a ghost.

"One spring about fifteen years back the weather was real wet. With all the rain we got the rivers were high and dangerous. River people watch out for high water, above flood stage. No sense risking your neck.

"Ratonia knew her stuff by this time, seasoned by experience. She took a private party of four on this very river, the San Juan. They were camped around the bend from here. They were scientists of some kind, on the lookout for rock art, ancient ruins.

"One evening she took a walk eastward off the river, following a gulch, a slot in the rocks that carries water out of the back country. She went off by herself.

"After a while the four people in camp heard a noise like distant thunder. They stood and looked around, startled and scared. The sound grew. Finally one of them figured it was water, a flash flood.

"They got into the boats and floated downstream, leaving camp just in time. The gulch exploded with waves of brown water, like Noah's flood.

In the desert, rain twenty or thirty miles up-country may run off into narrow canyon bottoms. Rain may not fall on the river, but it is still dangerous to hike in the gulches and side canyons that are river tributaries.

"After things quieted they paddled upstream. They could not believe the destruction, how the shore had been changed by the rush of floodwater. Their gear was gone, what they hadn't grabbed at the last minute. But they figured Ratonia was somehow okay. It was a big surprise when they saw her body floating into view just around sunrise. She was drowned, swallowed in flood water. Nobody could believe it.

River rapids are named by the people who run rivers. Treacherous sections of river become famous for how difficult they are, memorable events, or other reasons—like a can of rancid tuna that ruined someone's supper.

"Well, some weeks after she died, a young guide found himself in trouble on the Colorado, at a spot known as Rancid Tuna Rapid. He was raw, unseasoned, and he was about to hit the wall and flip. Suddenly he saw her, Ratonia. She told him what to do, and he saved himself and his boat.

"That first sighting was considered one young man's dizzy spell. Nobody says much about this kind of thing, a ghost, unless it happens over and over.

"The next thing you know she shows up again, like the first time, telling a boatman how to save himself and his passengers.

"Folks began keeping a record of the sightings. Stories have been fancied up, with different ideas as to what's true and what's pure invention.

"Some claim she's a canyon wren in shifted shape, because of that bird's sweet voice and how it resembles her own. Others will tell you she's a dipper, the water ouzel, a bird that takes kindly to swimming. People maintain they've seen her footprints, bare feet each time, in the mud on the banks. One old boat guide said he saw her floating along, chin deep, like she used to do.

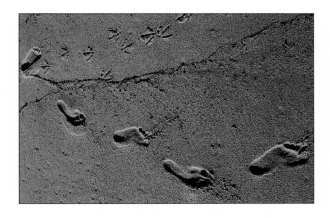

Wild places invite humans. People throughout history have made themselves feel safer in the wilderness by inventing protective spirits.

"She's on these rivers, there's no doubt. Call it ghostly if you like, she's around. Lives have been saved on account of her showing up and giving the right advice."

The old man stopped talking and silently puffed on his cigar. Nobody spoke. I half expected someone to say, "I don't believe in ghosts." Everyone present kept still.

I looked into the clear night sky and realized that the story of Ratonia was an invitation to dream and imagine.

Well before sunrise, by the light of the fading moon, I slipped into the river. The water murmured, cool and brown, around my legs. Stomach-down in the stream, I floated with my arms out, water lapping my chin the way the old man had described Ratonia doing it. I rolled over on my back. The water smelled like overripe melons.

I wished I would meet her.

You only meet her when you're in trouble, I reminded myself.

The currents in the stream were visible, evidenced by ripples on the surface. The tug and pressure against my body described where the strongest flow was, and the weakest. I understood how Ratonia learned to know the rivers by being *in* them.

At sunrise a heron lifted on broad wings out of the willows. Soon more followed. I realized I'd be missed and had to go back. After floating three miles I turned for shore.

I crawled out and at first could not make my arms and legs work. They were limp and weak, like rubber bands. Once my muscles were tightened, used to being on land again, I headed upstream to camp.

On the way back I thought about Ratonia, her ghostly appearances in the nick of time. Do ghosts exist, other than in our imaginations? There was a rustling in the willows. Was it she? Or a wild animal taking cover?

After hearing the old man's story, I saw the San Juan River with fresh eyes. Rivers, like people, are individual, changeable, mysterious. They have their own lives, personalities, and some, their own resident ghosts.

Crossing Water with a Dog

[This is a true story told to me by a friend.]

I didn't especially want to take the dog in the
boat, a Boston whaler. He was a gangly Golden
Retriever with an adoring nature and no brains, or
that's how he acted. I took him because my father,
on the dock seeing me off, said, "Take the dog." I
couldn't think of any reason not to.

The dog jumped joyfully into the boat. I was already aboard and was thrown sideways. I gripped the sides to keep from falling into the water.

"Down, Barnacle," I scolded. "Go sit. SIT!" I commanded.

His long nose wet and runny, his chin whiskers soppy with drool, Barnacle did as he always did in the boat, taking a position as figure-head, front feet on the bow, nose forward.

"You have money? The list?" my father asked.

"Yes," I replied, patting my back pocket, where two ten-dollar bills were rolled around my mother's shopping list. I was glad to be heading for town. On such a bright, clear day, with warm breezes on the bay, getting away in the small boat was pure pleasure.

I was twelve, young for soloing in the whaler, but I'd made the trip alone before. My family called it the "milk run." Dad, an experienced sailor, had taken me out in boats from the time I was tiny.

It was eight miles as the crow flies from Little Deer Island, where our house was, to the mainland—an hour's round-trip at most.

The whaler was fourteen feet long with an eighteen-horsepower engine, enough to propel it even in choppy water.

"See you later," I called, waving and turning my face toward the bay. Barnacle, eager to chime in with his own good-byes, snuffled in his throat.

I gripped the handle of the outboard, and we were off.

The water surface rippled under a light breeze. It gleamed with reflected light. I squinted against the glare and drew air into my lungs, loving the smell, the freshness.

"Not much wind today," I told the dog. "The water is a mirror. Wind must be one or two knots."

I always talked to Barnacle, carrying on one-sided conversations. He looked at me out of sorrowful amber eyes, lifting his head, twitching an ear, letting me know he heard.

I saw the familiar boats belonging to people we knew. I swung the handle on the motor, first right, then left, aiming for boats as if they were targets. I switched to the container-ship game, imagining that all the other boats had to watch out for me because I was the biggest.

"Small craft on the left, approaching windward," I said, using terms my dad had taught me. "Fishing boat on the port side."

I got tired of the game and pointed the bow toward town. Gulls swooped low, gliding in graceful arcs over my head as I came near the main docking area.

Seagulls belong to a large group of birds known as Herring Gulls. They are the scavengers of the coastline, eating almost anything. Seagulls rarely venture more than a few miles from land.

✳ The Beaufort Scale ✳

FORCE	SPEED knots	CONDITIONS
0	<1	Calm, sea like a mirror.
1	1-3	Light breeze, ripples only.
2	4-6	Breeze, small wavelets. Crests have a glassy appearance.
3	7-10	Gentle breeze, large wavelets, glassy foam, crests begin to break.
4	11-16	Moderate breeze, small waves, some white horses.
5	17-21	Fresh breeze, moderate waves, many white horses.
6	22-27	Strong breeze, large waves, probably some spray.
7	28-33	Near gale, mounting sea with foam blown in streaks downwind.
8	34-40	Gale, moderately high waves, crests break into spindrift.
9	41-47	Strong gale, high waves, dense foam, visibility affected.
10	48-55	Storm, very high waves, heavy sea roll, visibility impaired. Surface generally white.
11	56-63	Violent storm, exceptionally high waves, visibility poor.
12	64	Hurricane, air filled with foam and spray, visibility bad.

In 1805, Sir Francis Beaufort developed a thirteen-degree scale to measure the strength of wind at sea. Today it is still used for approximating wind speed. Speed at sea is measured in knots, or nautical miles per hour. One knot equals 1.15 mph.

I tied up and left the docks, walking up a side alley and along the main street of town. Barnacle followed, coming along slowly, his nose his guide.

"Come on," I said impatiently when he strayed. "You sure take your time about things."

The dog picked up his pace when I scolded him, until the aroma of a tossed banana skin and a partly eaten ice-cream cone attracted him. He sniffed at the bottoms of poles, the feet of mailboxes, curbs. His appetite for smells was bottomless.

With the groceries and the newspaper for my dad, Barnacle and I walked back to the boat and we headed back out into the bay.

I set the boat in the direction of home, Barnacle, as usual, poised like a guardian spirit at the bow, his nose in the air. This time I imagined myself a sailor in ancient times, alone but for a single trusted mate—Barnacle—on the vast sea, headed for a new land.

"The King and Queen have sent us on a dangerous ocean journey, to find gold and silver," I told the dog. "We have a map with empty spaces on it, for what is unknown."

I wondered if people in the new country would show us how to find fresh water, berries, fruit like coconuts and pineapples. I'd read about stranded sailors who survived on coconuts they shook off palms.

After a while, I changed the game. I was a South Sea islander from an even earlier time, piloting a canoe toward an island none of my people had seen but suspected was there. I feared many things, among them that my mate and I would fall off the edge of the world, which our people believed was flat. If you fell off, where did you go? Into empty space forever. Into nothingness for all eternity.

The earliest sailors never ventured very far from land, piloting by identifying landmarks on shore. Ancient navigators of the South Pacific created "maps" made of shells strung on tendrils of vine tied together. Each shell was a known island. The distance between one island and another was represented by the space between one shell and another.

"We must read the waves," I told Barnacle. "And watch how they lap the sides of the boat, the way they pass across the bow. At night we will find our way by the stars and the moon. We will notice the wind, and be aware when it changes direction."

I was dreamily immersed in my fiction that I was a voyager entrusted with a daunting task.

The spell of my imaginings was broken when a chill stroked the back of my neck, a cold finger of dampness. I shivered and pulled a worn woolen sweater out of a waterproof seabag on the bottom of the boat, slipping it on under my life jacket.

"A fast change in the weather," I said to Barnacle. "Thick fog coming in quickly."

Barnacle's tail, flagged with long hairs, brushed the air. He tilted his head, as if attentive to the hazy wetness moving in. He made me laugh. "You're good crew," I said. "A fine sailor."

I watched the fog come toward us. It spread rapidly, a damp, vaporous mist that germinated out of the sea and enveloped the world around the boat. I had not yet looked at the compass, and when I did the needle spun uselessly. I shook the small instrument, hoping to set it right. It was broken.

I knew we were off course. While I was familiar with fog rolling up the bay on winds off the Atlantic Ocean, this fog rose up as if made within the water itself.

I looked at Barnacle. Did he see something I could not?

I heard a buoy, a muffled sound in the heavy air. I moved toward it, hoping it would be one I would recognize. It wasn't. By its markings I knew we were headed out to sea.

The use of buoys and charts as tools for navigating goes back many centuries. The earliest charts displayed a compass rose, with radiating lines showing directions. Ports, landforms, submerged rocks, harbors, and shoals were also marked. Buoys of old might have been coconuts anchored with lines. Today's buoys are metal floats with bells, identifying numbers, and sometimes flashing lights.

Fog is a cloud that touches the ground. Fog over water is sometimes called seasmoke, and is dangerous to travel through. Lighthouses have foghorns to guide ships. Each lighthouse uses a different pattern of horn blasts, so captains will know where they are.

I peered into the gloom and listened to the smack of waves against the boat. The dog leaned forward, nose up.

Suddenly I saw land. It was not Little Deer Island.

Dismayed, I moved off and continued my search. More land came into view. Again, it was not my parents' island.

I wandered for an hour, fear growing, and then another hour, aware a person might be lost for days in fog, drifting ever further out to sea.

"Fog sticks around in these parts," I said to the dog. I felt helpless not knowing which way to go.

I looked at Barnacle. He always knew the way when we were on land. What did he know now? His nose was turned to the left side of the bow. Was this a hint? A clue?

I stared at him. "Trust a dog," I whispered. "Trust his instinct for homing in. Follow Barnacle's nose."

We have in our brains, as dogs and other animals do, a small unit the size of a sugar cube called the hippocampus. This organ helps us when we are lost, looking for the way back.

Experiments give evidence that this unit is triggered when we try to form a mental map of the space around us. The overall shape of the space that we recall, not the details within the space, allows us to become reoriented.

A dog's sense of smell is powerful enough that it can use its nose to locate itself, to smell the way home.

I made an abrupt ninety-degree turn to the left, the direction Barnacle's nose was pointing. I sensed the dog agreed with what I was doing when his tail wagged across the bottom of the boat. He was cheered by my move. Every bone in my body felt Barnacle had known the way all along.

Certain of nothing and everything at once, convinced I was right, we headed straight into the fog. For half an hour by my watch, we traveled ghostlike through the mist, the dog peering, as I was, in the direction we were taking.

When I saw the clock, the house, the familiar trees surrounding the house, the steps to the front door, I was filled with wonder and relief.

Three hours had passed. My father was on the dock, waiting.

"Where on earth have you been?" he demanded. "We've been worried sick about you."

"Barnacle knew the way home the whole time," I blurted. "He helped me find the way. We wandered all over. I was completely lost."

"What about the compass?" my father said accusingly. "Did you ever think of looking at the compass?"

"The compass is broken," I said, remembering how the needle spun as if loose on its pin.

"Never mind," he said. "I'm glad you're back."

It was some time before he was ready to hear my story, how Barnacle had pointed the way home.

Pig Voices
by Moonlight

On the edge of the mountain
A cloud hangs
And there my heart, my heart, my heart
hangs with it.
A TOHONO O'ODHAM SONG

"A great beast swallows the moon," I whispered.

"A giant creature takes a bite out of it."

I stepped cautiously in the gloom, half-blind from

tiredness and confusion, feeling my way through

thick brush and stands of stunted beech trees with

twisting branches. The trees, four and five feet tall,

The moon has always been a light to see by in the dark. However, moonlight distorts objects near the viewer, and also distorts distances, so a person thinks something is closer than it really is. It is important to learn to "see by moonlight" before using the glow of the moon as a source of illumination.

grew away from the prevailing winds coming off the Southern Ocean. The scrawny trunks pressed low to the slate-gray slopes of the mountain, as if wanting to lie down and forget growing upright.

Brilliant light from a full moon washed down the mountain. A lone cloud was passing over, the beast I imagined was eating the moon's round face. The wind was blowing. It was cold. It is always cold and windy in Tierra del Fuego, even in summer.

Blinking fires from numberless stars appeared to be flying away from the earth at high speed, an illusion brought on by fatigue, the weariness of a long day's hike, the yearning to be home.

I was hiking on a mountain Darwin had climbed, at the bottom of South America, one of several he wrote about in his book *The Voyage of the Beagle*. It was an old dream, to walk where Darwin had walked, to see what he saw in that remote, mostly unexplored part of the world.

It was too late to be on the mountain, and I was worried. More than an hour had passed since sundown. The taxi driver waiting for me at the bottom would be worrying. He might have given up on me, grown impatient, driven back to town. I wondered if he'd think to go for help. Perhaps in his concern for me, he had turned on his headlights, shining them into the night to help me find my way back.

"No," I said aloud. "It would wear out his battery too quickly." I was sure that even on a good day his battery was ancient, like the rest of his cab, a long, low sedan of unknown origin that rattled and shook on primitive dirt roads from the loss of crucial nuts and bolts.

"You'll wait for me, won't you?" I said pleadingly, as if the man could hear. "I know you'll wait. You'll snooze in your cab, figuring I know what I'm doing out here, after sunset."

Being in Tierra del Fuego came about unexpectedly, and I was determined to make the most of my brief stay. At supper each evening I'd look at a map and decide which mountain to climb. The cab driver picked me up at my hotel each morning. We'd drive up the coast through villages of pastel-colored houses. There were pigs in every village, wandering free, snuffling along the roadside. They moved in and out of the underbrush, snorting as they rooted around for something to eat.

They were big gray pigs, knee-high to me, with long eyelashes and friendly dispositions. Sometimes the driver tossed a scrap, a piece of his own lunch, and the pigs came running, gathering speed until they circled the cab. They lifted long, whiskered snouts and grunted eagerly.

Sometimes, when I returned at the end of a hike, a villager would be leaning against the cab—always a man, never a woman alone. On occasion children circled the cab. The children were responsible for the pigs in an informal way. They "herded" the pigs, although the pigs went where they wanted.

When I returned to the cab after a long day of trekking, the driver always had a smile for me, as if waiting was no trouble.

But I had never failed to return before dark.

As I tramped through the brush, I felt lucky a storm had not blown in, that it was not snowing, sleeting, or raining.

Storms along the coast of Tierra del Fuego are frequent and ferocious. Usually the higher you are on a mountain, the colder and windier it is. This is not so on these mountains. The wind is cold and blustery from the bases to the peaks.

The Tierra del Fuego coast is quite exposed. Ranks and tiers of peaks and ridges rise to two thousand feet, or three, or five. The winds, which Darwin called "impetuous," never cease.

Anything growing on the steep slopes is distorted by the never-ending winds into shapes and forms unlike what you see in moderate climates. The pounding winds give the mountainsides a brushed-back look, as if a giant had pressed the surface of the earth with the flat of his hand.

To traverse a hillside, descend into a gully, or climb over a ridge, the hiker makes corridors through forests of stunted trees and dense brush, channels beaten out with clenched fists, bent elbows, spread arms, and kicks from booted feet.

I had worked all day to circumnavigate the mountain. Somehow I had gone astray.

When the sun went down, and I was greeted by the rise of a full moon, my hopes soared. I would have light to see by. The moon would show me the way.

But traveling under the pearly influence of lunar light, I was even less certain of my direction.

The landscape of Tierra del Fuego, a true wilderness, is without trails, without directional signs common in more visited areas like the Swiss Alps, or even the Himalayas. After a week of hiking Darwin's Mountains, as I had come to call them, I had yet to see a cairn.

On this night, high above the rocky, wild shores of Cape Horn, I was without reference points. Below the equator, in the Southern Hemisphere, the night sky revealed to my untrained eyes an exotic display of stars in enigmatic clusters. I searched for the Dippers and Polaris, the North Star, but saw nothing I could name.

Weary and frustrated, worried about my driver, I dropped low into a tangle of scrubby underbrush when a cramp caught in my gut. Hunger or fear? I wasn't sure which.

I rose and continued on my way, listening to night sounds and the constant wind. I heard the rush of water and struck out in the direction of it. The roar of the wind merged with the rhythm of the new sound, but as I drew nearer, the noise of the water's torrent separated and became distinct.

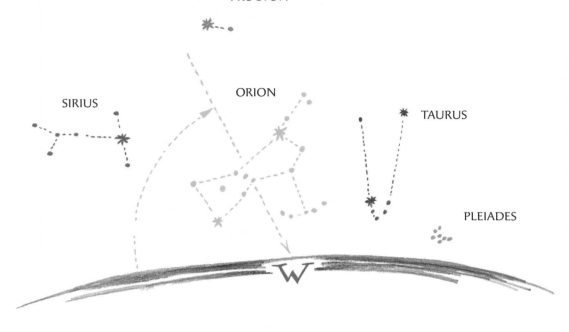

PROCYON

ORION

SIRIUS

TAURUS

PLEIADES

W

The night sky in the Southern Hemisphere is different from that in the Northern Hemisphere, seen above. The main constellation in the southern sky is called the Southern Cross, four stars that are always seen with the stars Alpha Centauri and Beta Centauri trailing behind. This illustration shows the path of the Southern Cross around the South Celestial pole.

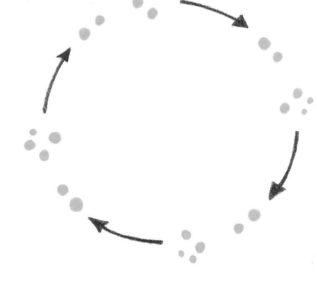

The river rampaged down the mountain in a rocky chasm wild and loud, like something demented. I decided to follow the river gorge down, to avoid the tangled thickets of low-growing forest. Already my jacket was badly torn from running into branches that seemed to leap out and grab me.

It was the "easy" way down. Crawling, scrambling, falling, and getting up again, I slowly made my way along the rocky banks. Deadfalls loomed, and I was forced to climb over them.

As I went lower, the world around me darkened. The moon's light, so gloriously reassuring before, was almost gone, dimmed by clouds, obscured by steep slopes.

I dropped down and at last came to a level dirt track ringing the base of the mountain.

By now the moon was of little use, but the sea was near on my left, the flanks of the mountain rose steeply on my right. I looked around to identify a landmark, anything to offer a clue.

The shape of the shoreline gave me some information, enough to convince me to turn southwest. I had recognized the sculpted shape of the shore, although I could not say how or why. Suddenly, I heard the soft, snuffly grunts of pigs.

"Piggy, piggy, piggy!" I called. "Where are the piggies?"

They came, hesitant at first, but then quite eagerly, brushing my legs, gurgling with gentle, persistent warmth. Their bodies let off heat. The chill of the wind was taken away once the animals surrounded me. I gave them little pinches of trail mix, all I had left.

I followed the lead pig, keeping up with it, loping at times to match the pace. We traveled about half a mile and there was the ancient cab and the sound-asleep driver.

I woke him and, as ever, a smile lit up his face.

"Oh, I was so worried!" he said in my language. "So worried, so worried, so worried."

It was a habit he had, to repeat everything three times.

"Sorry," I said. "Sorry to worry you. I got lost for a while. I took the river down. The pigs helped me find you."

"Eh?" he said, grinning and showing teeth stained by chewing tobacco. "Pigs good for something besides eating?" and he laughed at his own joke.

When finding your way, it is crucial to be attentive to even the smallest hints and clues that give direction—the way the wind is blowing, the drift of a cloud, smells, sounds, even pigs.

What Mr. Toad Knew

There's real life for you, embodied in that little cart. The open road, the dusty highway, the heath, the common, the hedgerows, the rolling downs! Camps, villages, towns, cities! Here today, up and off to somewhere else tomorrow! Travel, change, interest, excitement!

KENNETH GRAHAME, *THE WIND IN THE WILLOWS*

Mr. Toad, quoted above, knew a thing or two the others didn't, not Ratty, Mole, or Badger. He understood that travel is exciting. The open road is filled with the promise of adventure. Mr. Toad knew that, apart from picnics in the grass, cities are the best destinations of all.

The city of Toledo, Spain, built in medieval times.

Cities provide nearly endless sensations, so many that finding the way up one street and down another is a challenge. Figuring out how to navigate a city is more than reading a map or pinpointing directional signs. In cities there is so much to pay attention to that you have to decide what to notice, what to ignore.

In cities it is essential to orient yourself to up and down. Knowing what lies above, what sprawls below, helps to describe the whole.

The oldest cities tend to have important structures, cathedrals, forts, and government buildings on the highest hills. This way they were protected from invaders. The general populace lived in neighborhoods spread out on the flats below. In American cities, often designed after European cities, the same rule holds: When in doubt climb hills. In this way you are likely to arrive in the best neighborhoods rather than the most dangerous and derelict, the "skid row" neighborhoods.

To allow oneself to follow the general flow of humanity in a city is a way to get to know it. The market area is usually near the waterfront, if the city is a port. A transportation depot, such as a railroad terminal or bus station, is usually not far from the market.

The expression "the wrong side of the tracks" is based on the fact that the founders of many cities did not want industrial smoke and chaos near their personal dwellings. They plotted and mapped their towns in such a way that factories and rail yards were built well away from the tree-lined, well-groomed streets with proud mansions where the wealthy lived.

Cities may be built around rivers, since rivers are an ideal way to get from one place to another. Like veins carrying blood in the body, rivers are fluid pathways flowing to the sea, or into larger rivers. Rivers are avenues for commercial barges, ships, and other vessels.

Establish the location of the local river and you will discover that streets, alleys, and sidewalks radiate from the river.

The most ancient cities in the world were designed for foot travel, not cars, motorcycles, or buses. To accommodate modern travelers, city planners now decide which streets will be one way, which two way. It is easy to become confused about direction in cities constructed hundreds of years ago when you are riding through in an automobile.

Many American cities were planned to follow a grid system. Benjamin Franklin, the designer and city planner of Philadelphia, believed every square block must have its own park—a place to sit and read, feed the birds, or stroll with a baby.

Parks are important in cities, and in finding the way. From Mexico to Hong Kong, from Boston to San Francisco, town squares represent the "heart" of a city.

Begin there, perhaps sitting on a bandstand with your map on your lap, and return at the end of a day of exploring. Do not be afraid to become a little lost. It can be useful, jarring your mind into paying attention to the layout of the particular neighborhood you are in.

Another way to know a city is to establish, usually by reading a guidebook or map, where certain neighborhoods are. In Venice, for example, there is a section of town where cheesemakers have shops, and another where jewelers sell their wares.

A local market is a noisy, busy, crowded center of activity, and can serve as an memorable reference point for moving about the rest of the town.

Old European cities usually have ancient walls circling the inner city, the original part of town. The walls describe the limits of the town, or fortress, when it was new. It is useful, when exploring a city for the first time, to know where the inner city is and venture from it into neighborhoods beyond.

Some of my favorite cities have a port, a waterfront. Ports are especially interesting. There may be a rush of activity twenty-four hours a day. You hear languages from all over the world, and see flags from many different countries.

People, social beings that we are, relay information back and forth all the time. We are creatures of habit. The baker comes and goes from his shop at the same time each day.

Working men and women take the same bus each morning and evening. Women responsible for feeding their families make tracks for the marketplace. Being attentive to these comings and goings takes some of the mystery (and worry) out of rambling in a strange city. As with any environment, it takes time to become acquainted.

In a favorite neighborhood of mine, in a small town in northern California, I greet a certain parrot, an Amazon Green. It "flew the coop" some fifteen years ago. This bird has figured out how to live, how to thrive, in an environment foreign to its nature. It is the Chief of a local flock of pigeons. It bosses the pigeons around, now and then eating one for supper.

On summer nights, when people have backyard barbecues, it squawks and screeches, perhaps expressing its desire to share the food.

The parrot has a message: No matter how bewildering the unfamiliar environment may be to you, you might be able to make yourself at home.

Mr. Toad knew something the others did not, perhaps because he was bored with spring cleaning, restless as only toads can be. He understood the risks that come with entering unfamiliar territory. He took food, friends, and a proper means of getting from one place to another - the cart. Toad went prepared, and so everything, for the most part, turned out for the best.

Notes

Chapter I—Walking on the Jornada

Abbey, Edward. *Desert Solitaire.* A Touchstone Book. New York and London: Simon & Schuster, 1990.

Abbey, Edward. *Confessions of a Barbarian.* Boston: Little Brown and Company, 1994.

Boyles, Denis. *The Lost Lore of a Man's Life.* New York: Harper Perennial, a Division of HarperCollins Publishers, 1997.

Brown, Tom, Jr. *Tom Brown's Field Guide to Nature Observation and Tracking.* New York: Berkley Books, 1983.

Brown, Tom, Jr. *Tom Brown's Field Guide to Nature and Survival for Children.* New York: Berkley Books, 1989.

Chatwin, Bruce. *Songlines.* Elisabeth Sifton Books. New York: Viking Penguin Inc., 1987.

Ganci, Dave. *Hiking the Southwest.* San Francisco: Sierra Club Books, 1937.

Lawlor, Robert. *Voices of the First Day*. Rochester, VT: Inner Traditions International, Ltd., 1991.

Seidman, David. *The Essential Wilderness Navigator*. Camden, ME: Ragged Mountain Press, a Division of The McGraw-Hill Companies, 1995.

Warhous, Mark. *Another America*. New York: St. Martin's Press, 1997.

Chapter 2—Penguin Country

Cherry-Garrard, Apsley. *The Worst Journey in the World*. New York and London: Penguin Books, in association with Chatto & Windus, London, 1983.

Fejus, Claire. *People of the Noatak*. Volcano, CA: Volcano Press, 1966.

Halle, Louis J., *The Sea and the Ice*. Ithaca, NY: Cornell University Press, 1973.

Mowat, Farley. *Lost in the Barrens*. New York: Bantam Books, 1956.

Neider, Charles, ed. *Antarctica, Accounts from the Journals of Admiral Richard E. Byrd, James Cook, Edmund Hillary, Ernest Shackleton, and others*. New York: Dorset Press, 1972.

Spufford, Francis. *I May Be Some Time, Ice and the English Imagination*. New York: St. Martin's Press, 1997.

Wilson, Edward. *Diary of the Discovery Expedition to the Antarctic, 1901-1904*. London: Blandford Press, 1975.

Wilson, Edward. *Diary of the Terra Nova Expedition to the Antarctic. 1910-1912*. London: Blandford Press, 1972.

Chapter 3—The River Ghost

Davidson, James West. *The Complete Wilderness Paddler.* New York: Vintage Books, a Division of Random House, 1983.

DeVoto, Bernard, ed. *The Journals of Lewis and Clark.* Boston: Houghton Mifflin Company, 1953.

Ganci, Dave. *Hiking the Southwest.* San Francisco: Sierra Club Books, 1937.

Rezendes, Paul. *Tracking & the Art of Seeing, How to Read Animal Tracks & Signs.* Charlotte, VT: Camden House Publishing, Inc., 1995.

Seidman, David. *The Essential Wilderness Navigator.* Camden, ME: Ragged Mountain Press, a Division of McGraw-Hill Companies, 1995.

Stevens, Larry. *The Colorado River in Grand Canyon, A Guide.* Flagstaff, AZ: Red Lake Books, 1983.

Chapter 4—Crossing Water With a Dog

Note: Profound thanks to Alice Van Buren, the girl who crossed water with her dog. Alice related the story to me, and gave me permission to use it in this book.

Cline, Duane A. *Navigation in the Age of Discovery.* Rogers, AR: Montfleury, Inc., 1990.

Craighead, Frank C., Jr., and John J. Craighead. *How to Survive on Land and Sea.* Annapolis, MD: Naval Institute Press, 1984.

Sobel, Dava. *Longitude, The True Story of the Lone Genius Who Solved the Greatest Scientific Problem of His Time.* New York and London: Penguin Books, 1998.

Chapter 5—Pig Voices by Moonlight

Abbey, Edward. *Down the River.* A Plume Book. New York and London: The Penguin Group, 1982.

Brown, Tom, Jr. *The Tracker.* New York: Berkley Books, 1979.

Darwin, Charles. *The Voyage of the Beagle.* New York and London: Penguin Books, 1989.

Hertzog, Maurice. *Annapurna.* New York: E. P. Dutton & Company, 1953.

Olsen, Larry Dean. *Outdoor Survival Skills.* New York: Pocket Books, a Division of Simon & Schuster Inc., 1973.

Robinson, Arthur H. *Early Thematic Mapping.* Chicago and London: University of Chicago Press, 1982.

Chapter 6—What Mr. Toad Knew

Grahame, Kenneth. *The Wind in the Willows.* New York: The Viking Press, 1983.

Milne, A. A. *Winnie the Pooh.* New York: E. P. Dutton & Company, 1961.

About the Author

Jennifer Dewey grew up in the "wilds" of northern New Mexico, and at an early age felt comfortable finding her way in uncharted territory. Now a full time writer and illustrator of children's books, Jennifer still makes time for treks that take her far from home. This book is her expression of the wonder of how it feels to successfully find the way, even in places a person has never seen before.

About the Photographer

Salt Lake City naturalist, writer, and photographer Stephen Trimble has won awards for his writing and photography, including the Ansel Adams Award from The Sierra Club. His many books celebrate nature and wildlife. This is his fourth collaboration with Jennifer Owings Dewey.